Troubleshooting SFTP Connection Issues in AWS

Table of Contents

Chapter 1. Introduction

Navigating the complexities of network protocols such as Secure File Transfer Protocol (SFTP) can often be a daunting task, especially when it comes to AWS, one of the world's most comprehensive and broadly adopted cloud platforms. When the seamless flow of data is stalled due to SFTP connection issues, it can disrupt the harmony of your operations. This Special Report, "Troubleshooting SFTP Connection Issues in AWS," is meticulously designed to offer simple yet substantial solutions to such complexities. This instructive guide does not just share strategies to troubleshoot and resolve existing issues, but instills the knowledge and confidence to prevent future malfunctions efficiently. If SFTP connection issues have been a nagging pain point in your AWS infrastructure, this report could be the essential reading you've been looking for.

Chapter 2. Understanding the Basics of SFTP on AWS

Understanding the Secure File Transfer Protocol (SFTP) is a prerequisite for troubleshooting and preventing connection issues in an AWS setting. SFTP, a network protocol that provides file transfer and manipulation capabilities, is known for its security since it operates over a secure channel, typically SSH (Secure Shell).

2.1. WHAT IS SFTP?

SFTP is an extension of the SSH protocol, designed for secure file transfer. It provides all the functionality offered by FTP, yet bundles it with the security measures of SSH. Authentication of a client's connection to the server is handled by the SSH protocol itself, with SFTP then initiating file transfer over the established secure connection.

Unlike other file transfer protocols, SFTP encrypts both commands and data, preventing passwords and sensitive information from being transmitted openly over the network. This level of security means it's widely used for transferring large volumes of information between servers and cloud-based services, such as AWS.

2.2. ANATOMY OF SFTP

SFTP operates on a client-server architecture. The SFTP client interacts with the SFTP server to access, manage and transfer files. When a client initiates an SFTP session, it first establishes an SSH connection to the server. The server should be accessible over a network and should expose port 22 (the de facto standard for SSH traffic).

Once the connection is initiated, the SSH server validates the client's credentials, using either password authentication or public-private key pairing. After a successful authentication, an encrypted SSH session is created which serves as the channel for SFTP connection and secure data transfer.

2.3. SFTP ON AWS

Amazon Web Services offers AWS Transfer for SFTP (AWS SFTP), a fully managed service which enables the transfer of files directly in and out of Amazon S3 - a scalable object storage for data backup and analytics, using SFTP.

With AWS SFTP, you simply create a server, set up user accounts, and connect to the server using any SFTP client. The configuration and scaling are handled automatically by AWS, easing your administrative burden and simplifying the process of migrating your file transfer workflows to AWS.

2.4. CREATING AN SFTP SERVER ON AWS

You can create and customize an SFTP server using the AWS Management Console, the AWS CLI, or the AWS SDKs. First, you'll need to create a new SFTP server and assign an identity provider, which will be used to authenticate the end users. Then, you can add users by configuring their username, SSH public key, and an Amazon S3 bucket to store their transferred files.

Public endpoints for your server can be accessed over the internet, while VPC endpoints keep your traffic within the Amazon network, increasing the security of your data transfers. You may also choose to associate Elastic IP addresses with your server's endpoint for a static IP.

2.5. SECURITY IN SFTP ON AWS

Security in SFTP on AWS is inherently baked into the offered services. User authentication is managed by IAM policies and roles, allowing granular access controls to your S3 resources. The transferred data is automatically encrypted at rest in S3 and in transit to/from S3.

For additional security, you can configure logging for your SFTP server, keeping track of end-user activity and API calls via AWS CloudTrail. This allows monitoring and auditing of operations, helping you maintain compliance to your organizational, industry, or regional standards.

2.6. TROUBLESHOOTING COMMON ISSUES

As with any complex system, SFTP on AWS runs into issues. A frequent issue is failed connections, which are often caused by incorrect configurations, such as wrong user credentials, incorrect server setup, or misconfigured security groups and network ACL rules.

Aside from connectivity issues, file transfer problems can occur due to insufficient S3 permissions, improper formatting of an S3 URI, or an unreachable S3 bucket. In the next chapters, we will delve deeper into these challenges and discuss strategies to resolve them.

SFTP on AWS offers increased reliability and enhanced performance, all whilst ensuring data stays secure during transmission. To maximize this service, a good understanding of SFTP, AWS architecture, and common troubleshooting techniques is indispensable. In the upcoming chapters, we will build upon this foundation, focusing on strategies for troubleshooting and preventing SFTP connection issues in an AWS environment.

Chapter 3. Identifying Common SFTP Connection Issues

Before we unravel the solutions to the common SFTP connection issues faced in AWS, it's crucial to identify these problems first. This is essential in determining the perfect remedy suited for the different challenges you might encounter.

3.1. Overview of SFTP in AWS

Secure File Transfer Protocol (SFTP) is a network protocol providing file access, file transfer, and file management functionalities over secure channels. Implemented on AWS, SFTP provides a secure way to move files in and out of AWS S3 storage or EFS.

3.2. SFTP Connection Issues and Their Causes

Several problems could cause the inability to connect via SFTP in AWS. Some of these are:

Incorrect Credentials

Invalid credentials include problems with the SSH key pair, username, or password. The AWS Transfer Family uses Secure Shell (SSH) keys to authenticate connections. When the SSH key is incorrect, misplaced, or not recognized, it results in a connection failure.

To fix these issues, ensure that the SSH keys for the SFTP server are accessible and configured correctly. Additionally, verify that the

Transfer server authentication method aligns with the client's settings.

Firewall Restrictions

Sometimes, the problem could be as simple as the security groups or NACLs blocking the SFTP connection requests. This happens when the ingress rules for the security group or network access control list (NACL) related to your SFTP server do not allow connection requests from your IP address on the required port (usually port 22 for SFTP).

To navigate this, change your security group and NACL settings to allow ingress traffic from your IP address. Also, ensure that the server's listening port is open and reachable.

SFTP Server Down

Another problem could be that the SFTP server is unavailable. The server could be down because it's stopped, terminated, or facing issues.

Check the AWS Transfer Family console to determine the status of your server. If the server is stopped or terminated, you'd need to restart or recreate it.

Issues with the End-User Client

Sometimes, your SFTP client might have problems causing a failed connection. The issues could range from misaligned software settings, an outdated SFTP client, or poor network connection.

Ensure your client software is up-to-date and correctly configured. Also, verify your network connection to make sure it's stable.

IP Blacklisting

Your IP address might have been blacklisted unknowingly. AWS can block an IP address if it breaches certain security rules.

To resolve this issue, contact AWS Support to verify if your IP address has been blocked and to request for it to be unblocked.

3.3. Troubleshooting Process

While troubleshooting SFTP connection problems, adopt a systematic approach. Start by checking the client's configuration, then verify the server's status and settings. Next, confirm the network connections and, finally, reach out to AWS support if the issues persist.

Each connection problem is unique, but they have similar symptoms. Being aware of these common issues is a step in the right direction. But, knowing the cause helps you pinpoint the problem more effectively. In the subsequent chapters, we will delve deeper into each of these problems and provide specific solutions and strategies to diagnose and tackle them head-on. By understanding these common issues, you can better equip yourself to prevent them from arising in future.

Chapter 4. Investigating Network Level Issues

Network level issues can be a major hindrance to seamless SFTP connections in AWS. This chapter will guide you on how to investigate such problems and outline potential resolutions to them.

4.1. Understanding Network Basics

It's essential to revisit network basics and understand key concepts, as they form the bedrock of any troubleshooting strategy. Networks are designed in different layers in accordance with the OSI model: Physical, Data Link, Network, Transport, Session, Presentation, and Application. Different protocols operate at different layers. The SFTP protocol operates at the application layer. However, tracing an issue around this protocol may require investigating the underlying network layers.

4.2. Configure Security Groups and Network ACLs

AWS leverages security groups and network access control lists (ACLs) to provide security at the protocol and subnet level respectively. Wrong configurations in these settings can cause SFTP connections to fail.

To check if Security Group settings are causing the problem:

1. Verify if the Security Groups attached to your instance allows inbound traffic for SFTP. The SFTP protocol operates over SSH, so ensure that the inbound rule allows SSH connections (TCP Port 22).

2. If no such rule exists, create a new rule to allow inbound SSH traffic.

To resolve Network ACLs issues:

1. Ensure that the attached ACL allows both inbound and outbound traffic on TCP Port 22.

2. Check if there are any rules in the ACL that could be denying such traffic. Delete any such rule found.

Always test the connection after making any changes to the settings.

4.3. Examine VPC/Subnet Configuration

Virtual Private Cloud (VPC) and associated subnet configuration are also potential troublemakers for SFTP connections.

1. Confirm if the instance resides in a VPC that has internet access. Otherwise, the instance will be unreachable.

2. Check the routing tables for your subnet and confirm that they have a route to the internet or your local network, depending on which you want to establish a connection with.

4.4. Check Transport Layer Issues

The transport layer issues pertain to the TCP session establishment between your client machine and the AWS SFTP server. You need to validate if a three-way handshake is successfully happening, which can be confirmed through a packet capture approach.

Tools like Wireshark or TCPDump can be employed for collecting packet data. After setting up the packet capture, try to make an SFTP connection and analyze the data collected. Specifically, look for the

SYN, SYN-ACK, and ACK packets which represent, respectively, connection request, acknowledgment receipt, and acknowledgment of the receipt. Any missing packet or out-of-order delivery could suggest a problem.

4.5. Verifying DNS and IP Addresses

A mistyped IP or wrongly configured DNS could result in connection issues. Even discrepancies in private and public addresses or Elastic IP addresses might create problems.

1. To verify this, consider using tools like 'nslookup', 'dig', or 'ping' to confirm if the DNS resolution is working properly.

2. Check the IP address configured in your SFTP client, whether it is reachable and if there are issues with firewalls or proxy configurations at the client side.

4.6. Dealing with Latency Issues

Latency can impair the speed and quality of data transfer over SFTP. To diagnose latency problems, you can use ICMP ping to the AWS endpoint to gauge the round-trip time for packets. Remember that ICMP pings use a different protocol (ICMP) and port (ICMP does not use port numbers), so the results will not be identical to SFTP's performance but could be an effective indicator.

4.7. Ensuring Right Software Configurations

The client-side software configurations could also be causing the SFTP connection issues. You should:

1. Verify the SFTP client settings. Refer to manufacturer documents

for optimal settings.

2. Ensure your SSH configuration file (sshd_config on Linux servers) has the correct settings to allow SFTP.

These steps will provide a comprehensive framework for investigating network level issues when dealing with SFTP connection problems in the AWS landscape. The investigation process might seem intimidating at first. However, with detailed inspection and methodical troubleshooting, the grip on network-level issues can be strengthened, thus ensuring smooth and secure data flow across the network.

Chapter 5. Debugging AWS IAM and SFTP User Permissions

Before diving into the comprehensive details of debugging AWS IAM and SFTP user permissions, it is crucial to establish an understanding of AWS Identity and Access Management (IAM). This service assists in securing and managing access to AWS services and resources. SFTP User Permissions, on the other hand, govern the user access controls within the SFTP server. Together, they play an instrumental role in managing and regulating network communications.

5.1. Understanding AWS IAM

IAM facilitates the creation and management of AWS users and groups and dictates permissions to allow or deny their access to AWS resources. It's a core component of AWS security. Typically, issues regarding IAM come in the form of users not being able to access specific resources – this can happen because of insufficient permissions or due to misconfiguration.

Understanding how IAM roles work with AWS Transfer for SFTP (AWS SFTP) is key. When a client initiates an SFTP session, the service assumes an IAM role to pull the necessary access policies. If any issue arises during this process, the SFTP session won't proceed as expected.

5.2. Prerequisites for Debugging

Before jumping into the troubleshooting process, confirm that:

1. The IAM permissions policy assigned to your IAM role has

permissions to Amazon S3 and other required AWS services.

2. The trust relationship policy of your IAM role permits AWS SFTP to assume the role.

If these are not properly configured, connection errors may occur.

5.3. Troubleshooting AWS IAM User Errors

One of the most common user errors results from inadequate or incorrectly assigned IAM permissions. When AWS SFTP tries to assume your IAM role and fails, ensure the following:

1. Your role permissions policy should have all necessary access rights.

2. The role should be assumable by the AWS Transfer service. Validate this through the role's trust policy.

Here is a sample policy:

```
{
  "Version": "2012-10-17",
  "Statement": [{
    "Effect": "Allow",
    "Principal": {
      "Service": "transfer.amazonaws.com"
    },
    "Action": "sts:AssumeRole"
  }]
}
```

If the IAM role isn't assumable, correct this configuration and try logging in to the SFTP server again.

5.4. Unraveling Connection Issues with Detailed Error Messages

Utilizing detailed error messages returned by AWS Transfer for SFTP can be particularly useful when debugging connectivity issues.

Examples of error messages include:

1. "User username cannot be authenticated with any of the available methods." - Ensure that the Public SSH key is correctly associated with the SFTP user.

2. "Invalid request: the S3 bucket in your HOME_DIRECTORY element doesn't exist." - Verify that the S3 bucket specified in the user's home directory exists and is typed correctly.

3. "Access denied to bucket." - Verify that the IAM role associated with the SFTP user has the necessary permissions to the bucket.

5.5. Debugging Permission Boundary Errors

If your IAM role includes a permissions boundary, AWS SFTP cannot assume that role. You must remove this boundary in IAM. After the boundary removal, double-check the policy permissions as the policy might have changed during the removal process.

5.6. Evaluating AWS SFTP User Permissions

While IAM permissions focus on AWS resources, SFTP user permissions are centered on the SFTP server itself. Several issues can occur due to misconfiguration of such permissions.

5.7. Debugging Issues with Home Directories

Each user on the SFTP server gets a home directory, generally tied to a specific S3 bucket. If the user cannot access their home directory, ensure:

1. The S3 bucket specified in the home directory exists.

2. The IAM role tied to the SFTP user has sufficient permissions for the specified S3 bucket.

5.8. Analyzing Scope-Down Policies

In AWS SFTP, you can utilize a Scope-Down Policy, an optional IAM policy that further restricts user actions within an SFTP session. If the user is experiencing restrictions, check whether a Scope-Down Policy is active and possibly limiting access.

In essence, debugging issues with AWS IAM and SFTP permissions isn't a standalone process, and it goes hand-in-hand with the deeper understanding of IAM services, SFTP user permissions, and their interaction. A systematic procedure revolving around the evaluation of error messages, AWS IAM roles and permissions, and SFTP user permissions can decode the most common issues that have the potential to disrupt the harmony of SFTP sessions on AWS.

Chapter 6. Resolving DNS and Hostname Resolution Hurdles

Understanding DNS (Domain Name System) and hostname resolution is vital when connecting to a server via SFTP. This process converts a domain name or hostname like 'myserver.com' into an IP address, like 192.0.2.1, understood by network protocols. Problems with DNS resolution can negatively impact SFTP connections, disrupting the vital flow of information in your AWS environment.

6.1. Basics of DNS and Hostname Resolution

A DNS server stores domain names and hostnames, pairs them with their IP addresses, and provides these details upon request. Your client system uses its configured DNS servers to query the IP address corresponding to the domain name or hostname you're trying to connect to. If the DNS server can't resolve the name, the SFTP connection might fail.

6.2. Common DNS Troubles and Their Symptoms

Problems with DNS can pop up in a few ways. If the DNS server is not operational or can't be contacted at all, your client system won't be able to request or receive the vital IP address information. Also, incorrect DNS settings in your client system can try to query the wrong server. These issues can materialize as an "Unknown Host" error or a timeout when trying to initiate the SFTP connection.

If the DNS resolution is successful but in error (e.g., the DNS server returns an incorrect IP address), your SFTP client will establish a connection with the wrong server. The server might not respond to the SFTP protocol since it wasn't designed for it, or it will reject your attempted login if the credentials don't match their system.

It's worth noting that while these are common symptoms and potential issues, they can also stem from other problems that aren't related to DNS. Still, any time you're encountering difficulty initiating an SFTP connection, DNS should be one of the first areas you examine.

6.3. Checking Your DNS Setup

When troubleshooting a DNS problem, the first thing to verify is the proper configuration of your client system. If you're using a Unix-like system, the /etc/resolv.conf file should list the IP addresses of your DNS servers. For Windows, you can use the ipconfig /all command at the Command Prompt to see your system's DNS settings.

Once you verify that DNS settings are correct, you can manually use these servers to resolve the hostname. Unix-like systems can utilize the dig or nslookup utilities for this, and on Windows, you can use nslookup. These tools will request the corresponding IP address for your domain or hostname from your DNS servers and return any responses or error messages to help you isolate potential issues.

6.4. Fixing DNS Issues by Changing Your DNS Server

If you're experiencing issues with your current DNS server, one possible solution is to change the DNS servers your client system is using. Many Internet Service Providers (ISPs) operate their DNS servers, but they can have reliability or performance issues.

Switching to a well-known public DNS server, like Google's 8.8.8.8 or Quad9's 9.9.9.9, might resolve your SFTP connection issues on AWS.

To change the DNS server of your system, UNIX-like systems rely on modifying the `/etc/resolv.conf` file and adding the following lines:

```
nameserver 8.8.8.8
nameserver 8.8.4.4
```

Remember to adjust the IP addresses according to the DNS servers you choose. On Windows, changing DNS settings involves going to Network Connections, selecting your network, choosing 'Properties', and then 'Internet Protocol Version 4 (TCP/IPv4)' or 'Internet Protocol Version 6 (TCP/IPv6)', depending on which you're using.

6.5. Miscellaneous DNS Troubles

Some issues don't stem from the DNS server but from the information contained within it. For instance, if an incorrect IP address is associated with your hostname or domain name on the DNS server, the erroneously resolved address could lead to a misconnection.

Also, if your AWS server's IP address changes, but the DNS server is not updated accordingly, this stale or incorrect information can cause new connection attempts to fail. The solution to this problem is beyond the client; the DNS record must be updated on the DNS server itself, either manually by the system administrator or automatically through dynamic DNS mechanisms.

In conclusion, understanding the basics of DNS and hostname resolution is vital for troubleshooting SFTP connection issues. It helps professionals to locate the problem accurately and apply effective solutions to them promptly. This not only ensures the seamless flow of data but also significantly reduces the chances of future disruptions.

Chapter 7. Decrypting Encryption and Cipher Suite Problems

Understanding the intricate frameworks of encryption and deciphering cipher suite problems can provide valuable insight into SFTP connection issues within AWS. Through an examination of these areas, it becomes possible to recognize and resolve latent glitches disrupting your system.

7.1. Comprehending the Basics of Encryption

Source encryption is the cornerstone of secure data transmission, protecting content from unauthorized access. Consequently, understanding its principles is inherent for effective fault detection and solution.

An SFTP connection primarily rests on the Secure Shell (SSH) encryption protocol. This protocol guarantees the confidentiality and integrity of data, key generation, and key exchange between communicating parties. Here is a basic layout of how SSH achieves a secure connection:

1. Key Exchange Phase: This initiates the SSH communication. Both parties exchange some random numbers and use these to form a shared secret, which isn't transmitted.

2. Server Host Key Verification: After the initial key exchange, the client verifies the server's authenticity with its public key. If the server's identity doesn't match the stored one for that server's IP and port, a warning is issued, and connection may be aborted.

3. Encryption, Integrity, and Authentication Algorithms Negotiation: Both parties also agree on which algorithms to use for the session's encryption. This inclusion of algorithms translates into the primary SSH negotiation.

7.2. Identifying Encryption Problems

If an SFTP connection has issues, SSH encryption may be at fault. Here are some common conflicts:

1. Host Key Not Recognized: The client workstation may not recognize the host key of the server. It may lead to a termination of operations right after connection. This issue often surfaces when you're connecting to a server for the first time or when the server has undergone infrastructure modifications like a change in IP.

2. Unsupported Cipher Suite: If the cipher suite used by the SSH server isn't supported by your AWS SFTP, it could obstruct the connection. This usually happens when you are trying to use outdated or unsupported cryptographic algorithms.

3. Discrepant Encryption Mode: SSH has two modes, CBC and CTR. If there's a mismatch between the modes used by the client and server, it can hamper the connection process.

7.3. Decrypting Cipher Suite Problems

The cipher suite choice is central to a successful SSH connection, making any cipher suite-related problem potentially impactful on the SFTP connection. Resolving these troubles involves a two-step path — detection and resolution.

1. Detection: Most modern SFTP clients furnish comprehensive logs that detail each step during a connection's establishment. By examining these logs, it's possible to pin a failure down to cipher suite negotiation. If the logs show an inability to agree on a cipher, you've detected a cipher suite problem.

2. Resolution: After a problem is identified, it's time for solutions. Here are some remedies:

   1. Update Cipher Suite: If your current cipher suite isn't supported, upgrading to a supported one by AWS SFTP is crucial.

   2. Configure AWS Security Policy: AWS lets you select a security policy for your SFTP server. It is crucial to align this policy with the algorithm you wish to use.

   3. Update SFTP Client: Sometimes, AWS may stop supporting certain algorithms due to security vulnerabilities. If this is indeed the case, updating your SFTP client to a version that supports the secure and supported algorithms is prudent.

7.4. Enhancing Encryption

Ensuring the smooth operation of your SFTP connection doesn't stop with troubleshooting - prevention is equally vital. By regularly updating your server and client software, you can ward off glitches that outdated systems might trigger. Additionally, periodic validation and refreshing of server host keys can keep your encryption mechanisms robust.

We've explored just the tip of the iceberg when it comes to understanding and troubleshooting encryption and cipher suite issues in SFTP connections over AWS. By building upon these foundations, you can maneuver through the maze that is data encryption in cloud settings - enhancing the integrity, security, and efficiency of your SFTP operations in AWS.

Chapter 8. Tackling SFTP File Transfer Failures

The crucial first step when dealing with SFTP file transfer failures is understanding the root of the issue. Various causes can initiate such failures including incorrect login details, improper file permissions, or network connectivity issues. This section provides a step-by-step guide to identify the root cause and recommend productive solutions for each potential scenario.

8.1. Identifying the Issue Using Log Files

Log files are an essential tool in diagnosing problems in any system. SFTP or SSH (Secure Shell) provides detailed logs that can be checked in case of a transfer failure. Logging verbosity can be increased to obtain more information about the transfer process.

On Linux systems, the log files are stored typically in /var/log/auth.log or /var/log/secure. For Windows, use an Event Viewer to access SSH logs. Note that the location and depth of these logs will depend on the SFTP server's configuration.

Filter the log entries to the time the issue occurred. Look for entries containing words such as 'failed', 'error', or 'denied'. These log entries provide valuable insight into what may be causing the failure.

8.2. Highlighting Common Error Messages

Each error message indicates a different problem. Some common ones are:

1. `permission denied`: This often implies that the SFTP user does not have the necessary permissions to read or write to the directory. Verify the user's permissions on both the source and destination directories.

2. `connection refused`: The SSH/SFTP service is not running on the server, or a firewall is blocking the connection. Check whether the SFTP service is running and the firewall rules permit the SFTP traffic.

3. `connection timed out`: Your client's network is not able to reach the SFTP server.

4. `authentication failed`: The SFTP client failed to authenticate with the server, likely due to an incorrect username or password.

Understanding these error messages is one of the crucial keys to identifying and resolving the issue.

8.3. Authentication Troubleshooting

Authenticating to an SFTP server requires correct credentials: a username and password or SSH-key pair. If there are any changes to these credentials on either side, authentication may fail, and thus prevents the file transfer.

1. Confirm that the username being used exists on the SFTP server.

2. If using a password for authentication, make sure it's correct. Remember, passwords are usually case sensitive.

3. If you're using an SSH key, verify the following:

   a. Key Pair: Confirm that you are using the correct private key on the client side, and the corresponding public key is correctly set in the server's authorized_keys file.

   b. Permission: Ensure that the private key and the directory containing it have strict permissions, not accessible to other users.

8.4. Network Connectivity Troubleshooting

It's possible that network issues could be causing the SFTP file transfer failures. To verify network connectivity:

1. Test the connection to the SFTP server from the SFTP client using the `ping` command. If this fails, resolve the network issues first.

2. Verify if the SFTP server is running and listening on the correct port. On Unix/Linux systems, you can use the `netstat` command to confirm this.

3. Check if there are any firewalls between the SFTP client and the server, and make sure they are configured to allow SFTP traffic.

8.5. Resolution Based on AWS-Specific Challenges

AWS provides robust networking and user control, but problems may still arise due to security group settings or IAM limitations.

1. Inbound/Outbound rules: Check the inbound and outbound rules of the security groups associated with your AWS instance which runs the SFTP service. Confirm that you have allowed the necessary SSH access, usually in port 22.

2. Network Access Control Lists (NACLs): NACLs act as a firewall for controlling traffic in and out of a network. Check your VPC's NACLs to ensure they are not blocking SFTP traffic.

3. IAM roles and policies: If the SFTP server is using an IAM role for access to S3 or other AWS resources, ensure that the proper policies are attached granting the necessary permissions.

To summarize, patience and a methodical approach can go a long way when troubleshooting SFTP file transfer failures. The path to resolution will depend on the type of issue encountered. Understanding the different error messages, along with their root causes, can drastically reduce the time taken to resolve a problem. By effectively reading and interpreting your system's log files, you can gain insight into what is causing your SFTP failures and find corrective paths to suit each unique case.

Chapter 9. Interpreting AWS CloudWatch Logs

AWS CloudWatch is an indispensable tool for monitoring and logging system data. It collects important metrics from your resources that can later be analyzed to gain operational visibility and insights. AWS CloudWatch logs, in particular, are key to diagnosing problems with servers or software. The logs consolidate the messages and provide a chronicle of events for tracing issues back to a faulty line of code or misconfigured network setting.

9.1. Understanding AWS CloudWatch Logs

To interpret AWS CloudWatch Logs effectively, it's essential to first understand what they are and the information they contain. CloudWatch Logs are part of the AWS CloudWatch service, used to monitor your AWS resources and applications in real time.

CloudWatch Logs aid in collecting and storing logs from your resources, applications, and services. They assist in understanding the history of system events, examining changes that might have led to any operational issues, and debugging for problem resolution.

9.2. Levels of Logging

Logs in CloudWatch consist of different severity levels, including error, warning, info, debug, and trace. Each level represents a type of logged event. Error logs indicate problems that have prevented tasks from completing. Warning logs note events that aren't necessarily errors but could be. Info logs inform about system events or changes. Debug logs provide detailed diagnostic information useful for troubleshooting. Trace logs provide more detailed information than debug.

9.3. The Structure of AWS CloudWatch Log Events

The AWS CloudWatch logs' structure comprises three main components: timestamp, event message, and ingestion time.

- The timestamp is the time the event occurred.

- The event message is the detailed information about the event.

- The ingestion time signifies when the AWS CloudWatch received the event.

It's crucial to understand these components to interpret AWS CloudWatch logs effectively.

9.4. Locating CloudWatch Logs

After launching the CloudWatch console, you can find logs under the Log groups option. You can locate specific log groups by inputting their names in the search bar. Logs are stored in groups to denote that they have the same retention, monitoring, and access control settings.

Each log group contains multiple log streams, and each stream can be seen as a sequence of log events sharing the same source. For example, a log stream could represent a particular instance of a task running on your application.

9.5. Interpreting Errors in Logs

When diagnosing an issue, the first step usually is to look at error logs, which indicate severe problems that need addressing. Warnings also provide vital hints, particularly for proactively preventing possible future issues.

Reading log files involves looking at timestamped entries and following the trail of events. While the contents of these entries do depend on what's logged by your applications, generally, you should pay attention to the sudden shifts in behavior or any anomalies.

9.6. Leveraging Filter and Search Features

CloudWatch provides powerful features to search and filter log data, which immensely simplify log analysis. These features allow you to find specific log data based on terms, phrases, or values in your log events, providing you with granular control over your log data search.

9.7. Leveraging CloudWatch Insights

CloudWatch Insights is an additional tool that helps to interactively parse, analyze, and visualize your log data. Insights help you understand the patterns and trends in your logs, especially when dealing with large volumes of log data. Queries in CloudWatch Insights use a structured query language, with which you can search, filter, and sort log data, as well as aggregate log information.

Inspecting AWS CloudWatch Logs often involves extracting insights from excessive log data and interpreting error messages. With a proper understanding of the logs' possibilities and usage, you can turn CloudWatch into an efficient troubleshooting assistant that makes it more straightforward to pinpoint and resolve issues within your AWS infrastructure.

9.8. Setting up Real-time Log Monitoring and Alerts

One of the crucial features of CloudWatch logs is the ability to set up real-time monitoring and alarms for specific phrases, values or patterns. CloudWatch Alarms allow you to automate actions depending upon predefined thresholds and send notifications.

Setting up an alert involves specifying the metric, setting the conditions for the alarm, and designating the associated actions if the conditions are met. With properly configured alarms, you can substantially speed up problem detection and improve the resiliency and performance of your applications.

Analyzing AWS CloudWatch Logs effectively is key to maintaining reliable and efficient applications. By understanding, navigating, and leveraging these logs, you can both diagnose and resolve issues in your AWS infrastructure, and use the insights gained to prevent future complications.

Chapter 10. Creating Robust SFTP Error Handling Techniques

SFTP or Secure File Transfer Protocol is a network protocol that provides file transfer and manipulation functionalities over any reliable data stream. Despite its efficiency and wide usage, SFTP connections can suffer from various issues, leading to disruptions. Understanding how to create robust error handling techniques is crucial in maintaining smooth operations.

10.1. Understanding the Importance of Error Handling

In any system, errors can arise at any point. They might occur due to several reasons: network issues, improper commands, server malfunctions, and more. How well these errors are handled can determine the robustness of your infrastructure. In the context of SFTP, error handling refers to the abilities and techniques to efficiently catch, handle, and resolve SFTP related errors. It also involves the ability to raise meaningful errors and exceptions for the client, thereby simplifying the overall troubleshooting process.

10.2. Error Codes in SFTP

There are various error codes that the SFTP protocol defines. Each error code corresponds to a certain issue or a set of similar issues. For better exception handling, understanding these codes is imperative. Some error codes include:

- SSH_FX_OK (0): Successful

- SSH_FX_EOF (1): End of file

- SSH_FX_NO_SUCH_FILE (2): File doesn't exist

- SSH_FX_PERMISSION_DENIED (3): Permission denied

- SSH_FX_BAD_MESSAGE (5): Bad message

There are numerous other error codes under SFTP. Familiarizing with them allows for mapping of specific solutions for specific error codes leading to efficient error handling.

10.3. Implementing a Basic Error-Handling Mechanism

A basic error handling mechanism involves setting up exception handling blocks. These blocks could be nested as per necessity and must cater to all anticipated errors. Here is a pseudo-code showing a basic error handling mechanism in an SFTP implementation.

```
try {
  // Attempt SFTP connection
}
catch(SSH_FX_NO_SUCH_FILE error) {
  // Handle a scenario where requested file does not
exist
}
catch(SSH_FX_PERMISSION_DENIED error) {
  // Respond to a permission denied error
}
catch(All other SSH_FX errors) {
  // Handle all other SSH_FX errors
}
finally {
  // Code to be executed irrespective of whether an
error occurred or not
```

```
}
```

This block will ensure that most common SFTP errors are appropriately handled.

10.4. Implementing an Advanced Error-Handling Mechanism

While a basic error handling mechanism will serve well for common errors, an advanced system must be in place to handle rare, unpredictable errors. An advanced error handling mechanism involves setting up additional layers of error handling techniques that could include:

1. Deep Dive Logging: Register every small transaction and record all parameters, statuses, and error messages.

2. Automated Alerts: Design the system to send automated alerts and notifications in case of exceptions and errors.

3. Fallback Mechanisms: If SFTP connection fails, the system should be able to fall back on FTP or other transfer protocols.

4. Retry Logic: If the error is due to temporary server issues or connectivity problems, a retry logic can help.

5. Error Escalation: Some errors could be due to events like server failures or permanent data loss. Such errors should be escalated to the admin through the quickest channel.

10.5. Integrating Error Handling Mechanisms with AWS

To incorporate these mechanisms into AWS is somewhat straightforward. For logging and debugging, you could utilize AWS

CloudWatch. Automated alerts and notifications can be handled through Amazon Simple Notification Service (SNS). As AWS hosts network load balancers, one could set them up for fallback mechanisms, and AWS Lambda can be utilized to implement retry logic. To escalate errors, AWS Chatbot, SNS, or similar services can be used.

10.6. Testing Your Error Handling System

Once your error handling system is setup, it is necessary to test it rigorously. This ensures that it functions as intended during real-time scenarios. Testing could involve simulating errors by artificially triggering them and checking if they are aptly handled.

By putting together these pieces of an effective error handling mechanism, you would be able to handle SFTP issues in AWS efficiently. These techniques, when properly integrated into your AWS ecosystems, can increase the robustness of your infrastructure, minimize downtime, and guarantee the smooth functioning of your services.

Remember, a good error handling system is not the one that suppresses the errors but the one that appropriately exposes them so the underlying causes can be resolved. You now have the knowledge to not only handle but also prevent SFTP connection issues in AWS, becoming in due course, a bullwark guaranteeing the optimal flow of data!

Chapter 11. Maintaining SFTP Connection Health and Best Practices

Maintaining a healthy SFTP connection in an AWS environment is a pivotal task that demands thorough understanding and diligent actions. This involves leveraging the inherent capabilities of the SFTP protocol while taking advantage of various AWS services and best practices to ensure a seamless and robust connection.

11.1. AWS Transfer for SFTP

AWS Transfer for SFTP (AWS SFTP) is a fully managed service that enables the transfer of files directly into and out of Amazon S3 using the SFTP protocol. AWS SFTP works with your existing systems and software, with support for popular SFTP clients like OpenSSH, FileZilla, and WinSCP. Apart from its simplicity of use, it also provides robust security, scalability, and overall reliability.

To ensure the optimal use of AWS SFTP, consider the following process recommendations:

1. Always ensure your IAM roles and security policies are set up correctly. This includes setting up least privilege IAM policies to ensure that only necessary services have access to your SFTP endpoint.

2. Timely analyze and monitor SFTP logs using CloudWatch to keep an eye on the connection attempts, successes, and failures. This can offer valuable insights into any potential issues.

3. Regularly audit your SFTP users. User credentials should be managed securely and access should be regularly reviewed to guard against any potential security compromises.

11.2. Network Configuration

Proper network configuration is a necessity to maintain and optimize your SFTP connection on AWS. It involves managing firewall settings, setting up correct networking rules and ensuring your overall network is sufficiently secure. Here are some recommendations:

1. Using Security Groups: Security groups function as a stateful firewall for your instances. Only allow inbound connections on TCP port 22 for the source IP addresses that need to connect to the AWS Transfer Server.

2. Network ACLs (Access Control Lists): Network ACLs function as a stateless firewall for controlling traffic in and out of a VPC. They should be properly set to avoid any network communication blockage.

3. VPC configuration: Ensure that your virtual private cloud (VPC) subnet has a working internet gateway, especially if your users are connecting from the internet.

11.3. Troubleshooting Connectivity Issues

If you experience any SFTP connection problems on AWS, the following guidelines can help diagnose and resolve them:

1. Ensure the client is using the correct endpoint URL.

2. If a connection timeout occurs, verify that your firewall rules allow outbound connections on the ephemeral ports that the client is using.

3. If the SFTP clients report a "host not found" error, verify that the client can resolve the server's hostname using DNS (Domain Name System).

4. In case of a "connection refused" error, ensure that your security groups and network ACLs in your VPC allow inbound connections on port 22 from the client's IP address.

Remember, CloudWatch logs can be incredibly valuable in diagnosing connectivity issues. They provide detailed information about each connection request and whether it was successful or failed.

11.4. Implementing Robust Security Practices

Security practices are crucial for maintaining a healthy SFTP connection with AWS. Strong security policies protect your connections from attacks and unauthorized access, thereby ensuring the smooth flow of data and uninterrupted business operations. Here are some security practices to consider:

1. User Management: Regularly audit user access rights and de-provision users who no longer require access.

2. Multi-Factor Authentication (MFA): Implement MFA to add an additional layer of security during authentication.

3. Encryption: Use industry-standard encryption protocols to secure your data during transit and at rest.

4. Logging and Monitoring: Regularly log and monitor activities on your SFTP server to quickly identify any suspicious activities and anomalies.

11.5. Conclusion

Successfully maintaining SFTP connection health and utilizing best practices requires regular monitoring, careful user and security management, and efficient troubleshooting skills. Through the diligent application of these practices, you can assure the efficient running of your AWS infrastructure and avoid the pitfalls and challenges associated with SFTP connection issues. As AWS continually evolves its services and features, staying updated with its latest developments will help in maintaining a smooth and secure SFTP connection.

Printed in Great Britain
by Amazon

42505032R00030